This book is dedicated to five-year-old
Peter Oljelund
who asked me to write it!
Bertila

The Vasa saga
by
Bertil Almqvist

Bonnier Carlsen

Once upon a time there was a king in Sweden whose name was Gustavus II Adolphus.

He was a mighty warrior and in order to fight his battles on the other side of the Baltic sea he needed many ships. And because he was a King of the House of Vasa naturally he wished to have a fine warship carrying the name Vasa! And this ship should be the most beautiful of all!

With this in mind he sent for the Dutch shipwright Hybertsson who had moved to Sweden and ordered him to build a fine vessel that could be christened Vasa

Hybertsson at once sent out his workmen
to the Royal Forests of Oak, where they set up
patterns on the trees so that they could decide
which trees would be suitable for the different parts
of the ship. The sculptors likewise went out in the forests
to select suitable limbs for their figureheads and images.

And the timbers and planks that they sawed and chopped were no trifles either!

Look at Vasa's rudder for instance – over thirty feet tall!

Theese are the angle timbers for supporting her decks ...

here they are sawing out the deckbeams ...

and here the workmen totter off with one of the deck planks – the longest was over fifty feet!

Vasa was built by very simple means, since the shipwrights had no drawings or plans to work from.

When cutting out the ribs
— for example —
they had to scratch out
their own curves
by means of a big nail
attached to a rope
and fastened
at the other end
to a stake.

And while the hull
was being built
the woodcarvers
were busy
carving out
the lions
and
innume-
rable
other
images
which were
to adorn
the ship.
Here we see
"Martin the Sculptor"
and his merry men
at work on the main bow figure
— a huge, fierce-looking lion!

Vasa was born in Stockholm in 1627. Her "cradle" was alongside the Nybroviken bay, where the Strand Hotel now stands (see map) →
Here we see her just before she was launched and before her completion afloat. It was not until she was in the water that they raised her proud masts and built her stately stern with all its splendid sculptures. The lion figurehead was mounted and all the gunports were fitted with fearsome leonine visages to scare off the enemies!

OH, how Vasa longed for the water!

✳ Vasa's "birthplace" and its surroundings ✳

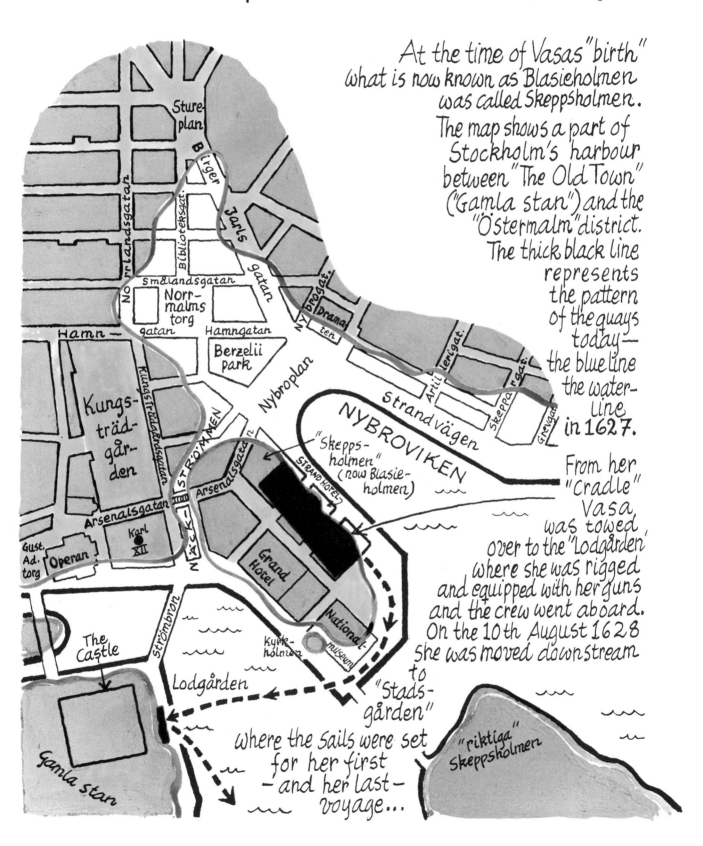

At the time of Vasas "birth" what is now known as Blasieholmen was called Skeppsholmen.

The map shows a part of Stockholm's harbour between "The Old Town" ("Gamla stan") and the "Östermalm" district. The thick black line represents the pattern of the quays today — the blue line the water-line in 1627.

From her "Cradle" Vasa was towed over to the 'Lodgården' where she was rigged and equipped with her guns and the crew went aboard. On the 10th August 1628 she was moved downstream to "Stads-gården" where the sails were set for her first — and her last — voyage...

Sture-plan

Birger

Jarls gatan

Norrlandsgatan

Biblioteksgat.

Smålandsgatan

Norr-malms torg

Drottninggat.

Dramaten

Hamn-gatan

Berzelii park

Hamn-gatan

Nybroplan

Nybro

Artillerigat.

Skeppargat.

Grevgat.

Strandvägen

NYBROVIKEN

"Skepps-holmen" (now Blasie-holmen)

Kungs-träd-går-den

Kungsträdgårdsgatan

STRÖMMEN

Arsenalsgatan

STRAND HOTEL

Arsenalsgatan

NÄCK-

Gust. Ad. torg

Operan

Karl XII

Grand Hotel

Nationalmuseum

Strömbron

The Castle

Kyrk-holmen

Lodgården

Gamla stan

"riktiga" Skeppsholmen

At noon on the 10th August 1628 Vasa set out on her maiden voyage. Her foretopsail was set, so was her foresail, her main-top and her mizzen ~ all bending before the southwesterly breeze, while the gulls screamed and the flags and pennants rippled gaily...

Look at me! cried Vasa to all the folk who had assembled
on the quays and up on the rocks round about. Look at me,
the grandest vessel ever built in the North! And true she was
as splendid as a newly-crowned queen! Her towering
stern, adorned with the emblem of the King and the
national coat of arms and a row of noble warriors,
glittered like a crown of gold and precious stones!
Never had a more magnificent vessel
moved through the Stockholm roads,
never had a more comely ship
set out for the open seas...

But – perhaps you noticed the dark cloud huddling and scowling over the hill in the previous picture! He was one of those nasty, jealous characters; the sort that produces a sudden storm just when you least expect it!
On this particularly August afternoon he had sat up there on the horizon and brooded over all the fuss and admiration around Vasa... All right! he growled to himself as she glided downstream – just you wait, my lady... I'll give you what for !!..
And suddenly he lunged forward and blew with all his might and main...

Poor Vasa was taken completely by surprise... She heeled violently over to one side, water gushed in through her gunports — and a few moments later her proud sails were dipping into the sparkling waves....

In no time at all the tragedy was complete. Filled with water — and already weighed down by her sixtyfour mighty cannons — Vasa sunk down into the sea : sail, flags, pennants and all... She came to a standstill on the seabed, nearly one hundred feet down, with only the tips of her masts above water....

And boats of all types and sizes hurried to the spot to save those on board...

So there sat Vasa, way down on the bed of the sea, in all her golden splendour. In those days the waters of the harbour roads were probably still so clear that you could make out the sparkle of the gold on Vasa's mighty stern and on the huge lion figurehead on her bows.
And they tried to raise Vasa, of course, but she was far too heavy with all her cannons. So they satisfied themselves with removing the tops of her masts, which were bound to get in the way of other ships within the space of thirty years moreover, the nails had rusted so that Vasa's towering stern toppled and fell in the mud...

No wonder poor Vasa wept great tears — though the tears rose — as big bubbles..!

Since Vasa
was too heavy to lift
to the surface again
they decided instead
to try to reclaim
her valuable
bronze cannons.
There was a man
called von Treileben
and he put
his head together
with another man,
a German called
Andreas Peckell,
who knew all about
salvaging.

Between them
in the year 1664 —
by means of a simple,
clever device
known as a
diving bell —
they brought up
fifty of Vasa's
sixtyfour cannons.
And while
they worked
the lions
on the ports
scowled their
disapproval!

When von Treileben and Peckel had hauled up as many cannons they could (nice of them to leave a few for us by the way!) Vasa felt much relieved — much more light-hearted. Why, I feel as if I could rise to the surface all on my own! she murmured to herself. Anyway it oughtn't to be so difficult for people to help me up now! And at nights she dreamed that she flew right up into the sky and shouted: Hello, Your Majesty! I'm here again!

That's what poor Vasa dreamed, but in fact it was to be centuries before it occurred to anyone to try and help her up. After von Treileben had retrieved her cannons in 1664 she was forgotten completely; left there in the mud to fall to pieces. A hundred years later not much remained of her former golden glory! The great yellow lion had jumped down from his place under the bowsprit, the cannon ports with their proud fierce masks lay spread around like autumn leaves and the fine oak planking was beginning to blacken...

Poor Vasa wept bigger bubble-tears than ever — especially now when even her eyelashes had floated away...

And the planking became blacker and blacker. When Vasa had been on the bottom for 300 years — until our century, that is — she was almost totally black. Furthermore the water had become so murky and nasty that not even the little fishes came along to say hello to her! Worst of all, meanwhile, were all the boats that came and dropped their anchors on her! And they didn't even take them away when they left, so that the miserable Vasa sunk lower and lower into the mud with all the extra weight of rusty anchors and chains...

Vasa watched in horror as the mud rose higher and higher around her....

But – just when things began to look hopeless...

One fine August day in 1956 two men sat fishing
in the murky harbour waters — oddly enough just over the spot
where Vasa had sunk in August 1628....

And suddenly
they got a bite!

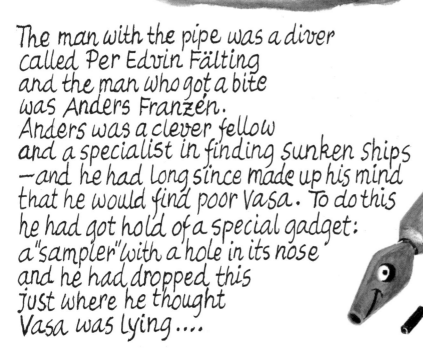

The man with the pipe was a diver
called Per Edvin Fälting
and the man who got a bite
was Anders Franzén.
Anders was a clever fellow
and a specialist in finding sunken ships
— and he had long since made up his mind
that he would find poor Vasa. To do this
he had got hold of a special gadget:
a "sampler" with a hole in its nose
and he had dropped this
just where he thought
Vasa was lying....

And
look!
When the
sampler
came up
there was
black oak
in its nose!
Franzén had
found Vasa!

Thus a few days later Vasa once again saw a human being — the first one for 300 years and more! Probably though she thought that diver Fälting was some sort of a big illuminated fish — since the people she remembered hardly looked like this one! This strange figure came lots of times subsequently, often accompanied by huge, black frogs that even swam in through her open cannon-ports! But not until these curious visitors began to dig tunnels under her tummy did she realize that something special was afoot — that perhaps they were going to help her back to the surface again!

Diver Fälting and Vasa soon became good friends. And when poor Vasa told them what an awful time she had had down there for over 300 years, Franzén and Fälting decided to help her up again. Yet how were they going to do this? They couldn't manage it by themselves! But Fälting was a diving instructor in the Swedish navy, and the navy very kindly lent him lots of skilled diving lads, who were the ones that dug the six tunnels under Vasa's tummy! When the tunnels were finished they pulled strong steel cables through —— and who do you think took hold of these cables and began to pull?!... None less than

ODEN and FRIGG

— the ancient one-eyed and bearded viking god and his wife! They heaved and they pulled and they heaved...

....And
at last!
On the 20th August
1959
Oden and Frigg
gave a special,
mighty jerk
and Vasa came out
from her bed of mud
and clay!

All of us who were there
could see that Vasa
was positively
bubbling over with glee!

In fact, of course,
"Oden" and "Frigg" were
what we call
salvaging pontoons
which the Neptune salva-
ging Co had sent along
free of charge
to lend a hand!

ON MONDAY 24TH APRIL 1961

the great historical moment had finally come when, after 333 years on the muddy seabed, Vasa stuck up a black fingertip over the surface to announce: Here I come!

And — thanks to the doughty pontoons — only a week later she had her nose above the surface!

Now Vasa was pumped out and secured with planks and scores of little wooden plugs (she even had her eyes protected against the bright daylight that she hadn't seen for centuries) and Oden and Frigg chugged off with her to the "Gustavus V dock" where she was to be laid up for repairs.

And, how Vasa enjoyed herself in the dock!

When the dock had been drained dry and the wooden supports were in place, she felt just like she had felt 334 years earlier. Now, as then, people swarmed and fussed all over her! Admittedly she was older and less elegant now, but at the same time she was, beyond a doubt, the very centre of attraction! In fact, if she heard aright, then she was being acclaimed "The Worlds oldest, fully identified ship"!!! ~ and was far superior to Nelson's "Victory" that had ruled the roost altogether too long on her stocks over in England!

Vasa enjoyed immensely being washed and brushed both inside and out and sprayed with fresh, clean water night and day! But the best fun of all was the archeologists who scrambled all over her and searched her from top to bottom! They pulled all sorts of bits and pieces which they placed in barrels and baths. Because Vasa was going to be restored and placed in a museum!

Thus in the year 1962 Vasa was "moored" in a temporary establishment known as the Vasamuseet at Djurgården.

But one day Vasa is to be given a more stately residence — a skyscraper perhaps — (it would have to be 200 feet tall!) where people from all over the world can witness what Vasa looked like when she set forth so proudly on her maiden voyage one sunny August day in 1628....

Perhaps a national monument?